AMERICAN
★ ★ ★
ICONS

3 4028 08185 4912
HARRIS COUNTY PUBLIC LIBRARY

J 976.403 Gol
Goldsworthy, Steve
Alamo
WITHDRAWN $12.95
ocn808215476
01/17/2013

D1219557

Alamo

Steve Goldsworthy

AV² provides enriched content that supplements and complements this book. Weigl's AV² books strive to create inspired learning and engage young minds in a total learning experience.

Your AV² Media Enhanced books come alive with...

Audio
Listen to sections of the book read aloud.

Video
Watch informative video clips.

Embedded Weblinks
Gain additional information for research.

Try This!
Complete activities and hands-on experiments.

Key Words
Study vocabulary, and complete a matching word activity.

Quizzes
Test your knowledge.

Slide Show
View images and captions, and prepare a presentation.

... and much, much more!

Go to **www.av2books.com**, and enter this book's unique code.

BOOK CODE

E169680

AV² by Weigl brings you media enhanced books that support active learning.

Published by AV² by Weigl
350 5th Avenue, 59th Floor, New York, NY 10118
Website: www.av2books.com   www.weigl.com

Copyright ©2013 AV² by Weigl
All rights reserved. No part of this publication may be reproduced, stored in a retrieval system, or transmitted in any form or by any means, electronic, mechanical, photocopying, recording, or otherwise, without the prior written permission of the publisher.

Library of Congress Control Number: 2012940120

ISBN 978-1-61913-080-7 (hard cover)
ISBN 978-1-61913-299-3 (soft cover)

Printed in the United States of America in North Mankato, Minnesota
1 2 3 4 5 6 7 8 9   16 15 14 13 12

052012
WEP050412

Editor: Aaron Carr   Design: Mandy Christiansen

Photo Credits
Every reasonable effort has been made to trace ownership and to obtain permission to reprint copyright material. The publishers would be pleased to have any errors or omissions brought to their attention so that they may be corrected in subsequent printings.

Weigl acknowledges Getty Images as the primary image supplier for this title.

CONTENTS

What is the Alamo?

The Alamo was the place of an important battle. The battle was fought between Mexico and Texas.

BONHAM

BOW

A National Symbol

Soldiers from Texas and the United States fought together at the battle. These soldiers fought for freedom. People say, "Remember the Alamo" to honor them.

How did the Alamo get its Name?

The Alamo was named after a tree that grows in Texas. The tree is called the *álamo.*

Where is the Alamo?

The Alamo is in Texas. Texas was once part of Mexico. It later became part of the United States.

Why was the Alamo Built?

The Alamo was built to be a mission. A mission is a place that has a small church and houses where priests live.

13

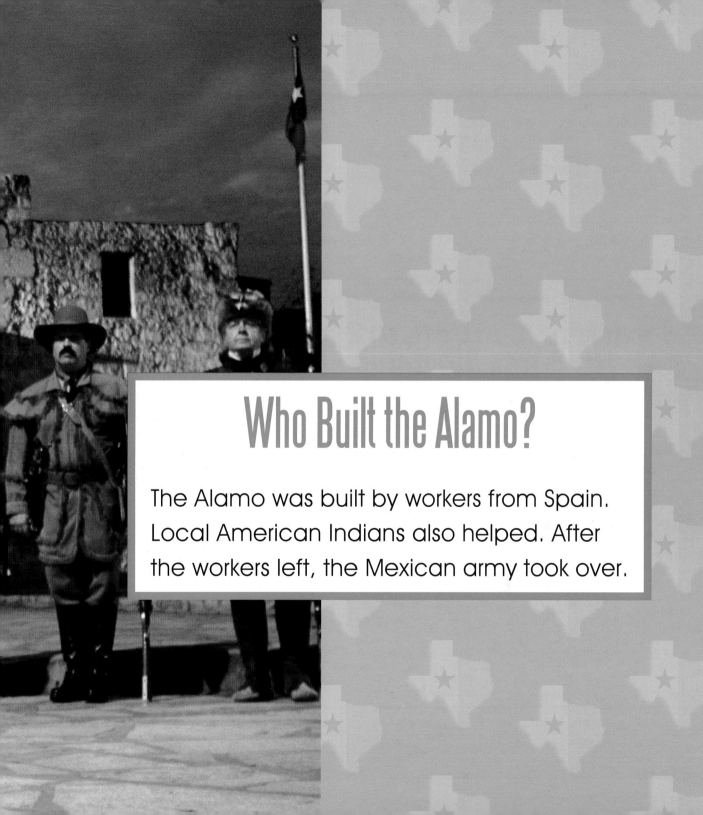

Who Built the Alamo?

The Alamo was built by workers from Spain. Local American Indians also helped. After the workers left, the Mexican army took over.

What was the Battle of the Alamo?

The Battle of the Alamo was fought for the freedom of Texas. The battle went on for 13 days.

Who were the Famous People at the Battle of Alamo?

Some famous people fought in the Battle of the Alamo. One of them was Davy Crockett. He is a famous folk hero.